SHANGH

THE CITY AT A (

Suzhou Creek
This historic shipping ro
the city, starting at The Bund and passing the
gallery district, 50 Moganshan Lu (see p063).

Shimao International Plaza
The huge Le Royal Méridien hotel is ensconced
in the 48 upper floors of this futuristic tower,
which anchors People's Park and Nanjing Lu.
789 Nanjing Donglu

Oriental Pearl TV Tower
Despite all the manic construction, this 468m
ball on a spike, built in 1995, is still Shanghai's
defining landmark, oozing technocratic glam.
See p024

Urban Planning Exhibition Center
Head here to view the future: a large-scale
model of the city as it could look in 2020.
See p024

Shanghai Tower
The second tallest building in the world when
it opened in 2015 has views that stretch for
up to 50km from the deck on the 120th floor.
See p012

Shanghai Museum
Wildly popular, this museum houses a fine
collection of Chinese artefacts and antiques,
and rather appropriately resembles a giant
cauldron with handles on all four sides.
201 Renmin Dadao

Concert Hall
Opened in 1930, the 1,200-seat concert hall
is part of the cluster of cultural buildings in
People's Park. It was lifted and moved 66.4m
in 2002 to make way for the adjacent highway.
523 Yan'an Donglu

INTRODUCTION
THE CHANGING FACE OF THE URBAN SCENE

Modern Shanghai is the calling card of China's intense economic development, the pounding heart of a ravenous consumerist body. At sundry points in history, it has been the biggest metropolis in the world, and today it is growing at a formidable rate. The continual construction fuelled by big government investment is astonishing. Stand on The Bund to take in Pudong's thrusting skyline, and it is hard to believe that 25 years ago, this was all green fields.

Then again, Shanghai's story has always been one of extreme reinventions. Divided into colonial concessions in the 1920s and 1930s, the chaotic, cosmopolitan milieu gave rise to new Chinese art forms, including cinema, animation and popular music. The 1950s and 1960s saw it transformed into an industrial centre and become a leftist revolutionary base during the Maoist era. By the late 1980s, it was furiously searching for its modern self.

The result is a highly ambitious and impatient city with a slight identity crisis. Its *longtang* neighbourhoods and art deco heritage are flattened to make way for progress one minute, and reworked back into the mix as design inspiration the next – large projects such as Xintiandi awkwardly straddle the ancient and modern. A burgeoning art scene has led to a spate of museum openings, but whether they can fill their walls and build legitimate collections is debatable. Meanwhile, Shanghai simply surges on, the epitome of Chinese urbanisation, its psyche growing ever more complex.

ESSENTIAL INFO
FACTS, FIGURES AND USEFUL ADDRESSES

TOURIST OFFICE
Huangpu District Service Centre
136 Chengdu Nanlu
T 5386 1882
www.meet-in-shanghai.net

TRANSPORT
Airport transfer to city centre
The Shanghai Maglev Train departs
regularly from Pudong International
Airport to Longyang Lu from around
7am until 9.45pm. The journey takes
8 minutes (¥50). From here you can
catch Metro Line 2 to People's Park
Metro
A one-day pass costs ¥18; a three-day
pass costs ¥45; a Maglev single trip and
one-day pass costs ¥55. Trains run until
11.30pm daily
Taxis
It's best to download the WeChat app and
use its cab-hailing service

EMERGENCY SERVICES
Ambulance
T 120
Fire
T 119
Police
T 110
Late-night pharmacy (until 9.30pm)
Hua Shi
1376 Nanjing Xilu
T 6279 8090

CONSULATES
British Consulate-General
The British Centre
17f Garden Square
968 Beijing Xilu
T 3279 2000
www.gov.uk

US Consulate
1469 Huai Hai Zhonglu
T 6433 6880
shanghai.usembassy-china.org.cn

POSTAL SERVICES
Post office
250 Beisuzhou Lu
T 6306 3972

BOOKS
New China, New Art by Richard Vine
(Prestel)
Shanghai by Alan Balfour and Zheng
Shiling (Wiley-Academy)
**Shanghai: The Rise and Fall of a
Decadent City 1842-1949** by Stella Dong
(HarperCollins)

WEBSITE
Newspaper
www.shanghaidaily.com

EVENTS
Design Shanghai
www.designshowshanghai.com
Shanghai Art Fair
www.sartfair.com
Shanghai Biennale
www.shanghaibiennale.org/en

COST OF LIVING
Taxi from airport to Fuxing Park
¥300
Cappuccino
¥35
Packet of cigarettes
¥20
Daily newspaper
¥1
Bottle of champagne
¥1,000

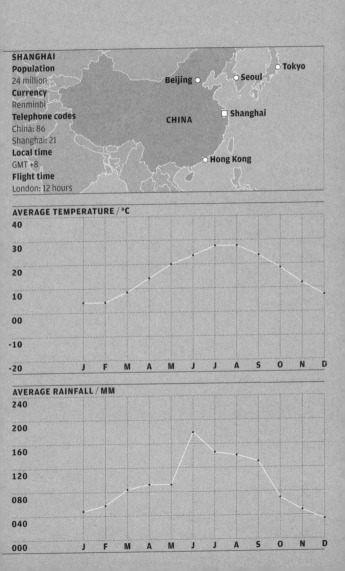

SHANGHAI
Population
24 million
Currency
Renminbi
Telephone codes
China: 86
Shanghai: 21
Local time
GMT +8
Flight time
London: 12 hours

Beijing ○
Seoul ○
Tokyo ○
CHINA
□ Shanghai
○ Hong Kong

AVERAGE TEMPERATURE / °C

40												
30												
20												
10												
00												
-10												
-20	J	F	M	A	M	J	J	A	S	O	N	D

AVERAGE RAINFALL / MM

240												
200												
160												
120												
080												
040												
000	J	F	M	A	M	J	J	A	S	O	N	D

NEIGHBOURHOODS
THE AREAS YOU NEED TO KNOW AND WHY

To help you navigate the city, we've chosen the most interesting districts (see below and the map inside the back cover) and colour-coded our featured venues, according to their location; those venues that are outside these areas are not coloured.

JING'AN

Business appointments might take you to Nanjing Xilu, a main artery of white-collar Shanghai. Here you will find lager-fuelled bar strips and huge glass-and-steel office towers, as well as John Portman's Shanghai Centre (1376 Nanjing Xilu, T 6279 8600), which is home to The Portman Ritz-Carlton (see p016). To the north is Suzhou Creek, a waterfront belt of sagging old industry and bohemian resettlement.

XINTIANDI

This olde-worlde mall of boutiques and eateries, including T8 (8 Xintiandi Beilu, Lane 181, Taicang Lu, T 6355 8999) and Yè Shanghai (see p051), assisted in teaching the city's developers the market logic of restoration, albeit in a controversial way. The Ben Wood-designed Xintiandi wiped out the old *longtang*, the brick tenements unique to early 20th-century Shanghai, to put up new ones, displacing thousands.

THE BUND

A riverside strip that is the legacy of the Opium Wars, built by the Brits and their allies along the arc of the Huangpu. The remaining facades of that era, which are mostly from the 1920s and 1930s, were the public face of the banking and nightlife centre of the concession. Party cadres and state banks have moved in, as have Western fashion empires. Venues such as Three on the Bund's Unico (see p032) make the most of the super views.

FRENCH CONCESSION

The area was first marked off in 1849 (after the British and Americans had settled here, but before the Japanese arrived) and sprawled west from the old Chinese city. Huge swathes are now gone, but the character of 'Frenchtown' persists. Cool concept stores, cafés, and nightspots, such as Liquid Laundry (see p038), Taste (see p052) and Triple-Major (see p085), dial up the hip factor.

PUDONG

Meaning 'east of the Huangpu', Pudong was predominantly farmland until the early 1990s. It now stands as a model of how a state-lubricated economic machine has wrought cityscapes out of mega-malls, office spires and development zones. But this is the only one with a £3bn mega-tower (see p012), an airport designed by Paul Andreu, and a giant antenna (see p024) that looks as if it landed from Mars.

PEOPLE'S PARK

For a century from the 1850s, this was the city's hippodrome, the site of derbies and polo. Today, it is both the civic centre and a recreational and cultural hub, thanks to Jean-Marie Charpentier's Grand Theatre (see p013) and MOCA (see p024), which is set in an artificial lake, and surrounded by architectural icons from every era. The stretch of Nanjing Donglu that leads from here to The Bund is a distinctly Chinese rendition of a pedestrian arcade.

LANDMARKS

THE SHAPE OF THE CITY SKYLINE

Downtown Shanghai is by far the most rewarding city in China to cover by foot, whether you stroll along the hyperactive Nanjing Lu, the riverside Bund promenade or the winding avenues of former colonial neighbourhoods. For those more used to rectilinear blocks, however, navigating can prove a challenge. Unlike Beijing, which khans and emperors outlined nearly a millennium ago, modern Shanghai has emerged only in the past 160 years – it had too many masterminds and too little time to devise a master plan.

Start with the basics – the Huangpu river splits the city in two. Pudong, the east bank, is where the last decade's main skyscrapers have gone up, including the dizzying Shanghai Tower (see p012). In the west, downtown is criss-crossed by two elevated highways and spread over three districts: Jing'an, a financial hub anchored by the Kerry Centre (1515 Nanjing Xilu); Huangpu, extending from People's Park down to the manicured Xintiandi; and Xuhui, which encompasses the French Concession and Xujiahui's chaotic malls.

As the city grows, its points of interest have sprawled. An arts district has cropped up at Moganshan Lu in the north-west, and West Bund, once an airport in the southern perimeter, has been transformed by an 11km strip of museums and galleries (see p056). Wujiaochang (see p014), a hectic junction given the Times Square treatment, holds down the north and university district.

For full addresses, see Resources.

Nanpu Bridge

One of two major city bridges crossing the Huangpu, this gigantic cable-stayed structure supported by H-shaped piles spans 423m of water at a height of 46m. Opened in 1991, it facilitated Pudong's upward surge. Its cantilevered spiralling approach system, likened to a dragon's tail (of course), minimises the land used and corkscrews up for outstanding views. *1410 Nanma Lu (tourist office)*

Shanghai Tower

It took just six years to top out the 632m of Gensler's twisting superstructure. It forms a muscular triumvirate with the Shanghai World Financial Center (SWFC) and Jin Mao Tower (left) that are representative of the city's hyper-lapse growth – 20 years ago, this area was mostly farmland. Shanghai Tower is distinctive for its double facade. The exterior layer rotates 120 degrees as it rises, while the spaces in-between form sky gardens, reached by lifts that cruise its 121 storeys at a speedy 40mph. Kohn Pedersen Fox's 492m SWFC was unveiled in 2008 capped by a circular void, but it was changed to a trapezoid (it's known as the 'Bottle-Opener') to avoid comparisons with Japan's rising sun symbol. SOM's 1999 Jin Mao is the most accomplished of the trio, taking its cues from a Chinese pagoda. *479 Lujiazui Huan Lu, T 2065 6800*

Tomorrow Square

This thrusting rocket ship of a skyscraper has loomed 285m above Nanjing Lu since 2003. It was designed by John Portman & Associates, who rotated the plan of the aluminium and glass tower by 45 degrees at the 37th floor to create its distinctive form and reflect the change of function between the apartments below and the JW Marriott hotel (T 5359 4969) in the upper part. It culminates in a pincer-like apex, the four pointed corners encasing a giant sphere, which appears jewel-like when lit up at night. Below, in People's Park, is Jean-Marie Charpentier's Grand Theatre (T 6386 8686). Before Beijing's march to the 2008 Olympics, it was the nexus of China's East meets West frenzy, a demonstration of the redemptive power of modern architecture. Now, it just seems rather quaint.
399 Nanjing Xilu

Wujiaochang

Under the Kuomintang (Nationalist Party of China) government's plan of the 1920s, Wujiaochang, which means Five Corners Plaza, was destined to be the heart of the metropolis. That never materialised, but today it is the lively commercial hub of Yangpu to the north, where you will find the Fudan and Tongji university campuses. The 100m-wide ellipsoid, which is a steel frame clad with aluminium, was conceived by urban designer Zhong Song to facilitate the intersection of the elevated highway, road junction and metro, while preserving the location as a public nucleus. The result is an expansive sunken pedestrian plaza shaded by the neon-lit underbelly of the viaduct. A clever circular water feature absorbs the noise of traffic passing above. Visit after dark when Song's orb becomes a futuristic mass of coloured lights.

HOTELS

WHERE TO STAY AND WHICH ROOMS TO BOOK

The scene has matured in the last decade, with numerous deluxe five-stars launching along with a clutch of boutique choices. Pick your accommodation by district as each locale has its advantages. Pudong's vertiginous Park Hyatt (see p021) and Shangri-La (33 Fu Cheng Lu, T 6882 8888) have the most coveted views. Facing them across the river, The Peninsula (see p020) and Waldorf Astoria (2 Zhongshan Dong Yi Lu, T 6322 9988) cater for The Bund.

In Xintiandi, two Kohn Pedersen Fox-designed towers house the chic Langham (99 Madang Lu, T 2330 2288) and Andaz (88 Songshan Lu, T 2310 1234), both popular with locals for weekend brunch. In Jing'An, The Portman Ritz-Carlton (1376 Nanjing Xilu, T 6279 8888) is the original grande dame, while the stylish PuLi Hotel and Spa (1 Changde Lu, T 3203 9999) has dragon-themed screens and ornate bronze in an otherwise sparse decor. For the French Concession experience, Mario Botta's Twelve at Hengshan (12 Hengshan Lu, T 3338 3888) is an anomaly amid the lanehouses, an oblong giant faced in terracotta tiles that encloses an elliptical garden, below which sits a pool softly illuminated by shafts of sun.

There is a more intimate experience to be had at designer digs Cachet (see p022) and Urbn (see p023), Swatch Art Peace Hotel (opposite) and perennial favourite The Waterhouse (see p018), a concrete shell repurposed into slick lodgings in South Bund. *For full addresses and room rates, see Resources.*

The Swatch Art Peace Hotel

This century-old landmark, originally the Palace Hotel, held the First International Opium Commission and hosted Chiang Kai-shek and Soong Mei-ling's engagement party in 1927. It was boldly reinvented as a hotel/arts project by the Swatch Group in 2011. Its 18 sleek live-work apartments are rented for six-month tenures, with artists requested to donate a piece to the hotel's collection, which is displayed throughout and in an on-site gallery. Seven rooms for regular guests have interiors by Parisian studio Jouin Manku. The Happiness Suite features a bed framed by a cane bird's nest and an inkwell bath between silk screens, and the Peace Suite (above) has a clubby vibe and a retro-futuristic bathroom set in a centrepiece swirl of sculptural elm wood. *23 Nanjing Donglu, T 2329 8500, www.swatch-art-peace-hotel.com*

The Waterhouse
Local architects Neri&Hu transformed
a 1930s Japanese army HQ in the docks
into an industrial-glam boutique pad,
fusing the framework (steel supports,
concrete walls) with design classics and
high-tech gizmos. Each of the 19 bright
rooms has a slightly different layout; we
liked the Courtyard Suite (pictured) for
its cheeky bedside glass-enclosed tub.
1-3 Maojiayuan Lu, T 6080 2988

The Peninsula

Its prime riverside address overlooking the gardens of the old British Consulate and the art deco-inspired Pierre Yves-Rochon design have been grabbing the headlines since 2009, but it's the details that make the experience here. A calming palette is complemented by black lacquer, restored brass finishes and hand-painted wallpaper, and there are fireplaces, dressing rooms, humidity control and valet boxes in all 235 rooms; Deluxe River Suites (above) have knockout views. Two of the five restaurants are Michelin-starred – Cantonese Yi Long Court (T 2327 6742), where the chef's table has an aerial-view cam trained on Tang Chi Keung, and Sir Elly's (T 2327 6756), which specialises in French cuisine. Its bar, up on the roof, has a jaw-dropping panorama.
32 Zhongshan Dong Yi Lu, T 2327 2888, www.peninsula.com

Park Hyatt

In a city of superlatives, the Park Hyatt is one of the highest hotels in the world, spanning floors 79 to 93 of the 101-storey SWFC (see p012). Guests are whisked via express elevator to the 87th-floor lobby, which looks down on all around it. The establishment has just about everything you could possibly want in one building, including the Water's Edge spa, with a 20m infinity pool and t'ai chi courtyard, as well as three restaurants; among them is 100 Century Avenue (T 6888 1234), dishing up Chinese, Japanese and Western cuisine via wok and sushi stations and a wood-fired pizza oven. The 174 guest rooms have been given a modern Asian fit-out by Tony Chi. The Chairman Suite (above) has 180-degree vistas over the river and The Bund.

100 Century Avenue, T 6888 1234,
www.parkhyattshanghai.com

Cachet Boutique

The 2014 takeover of JIA hotel by Hong Kong's Cachet Group saw a refurbishment of the rooms by New York-based fashion designer Jay Godfrey, who has given the property a glitzier feel, from the gold-tiled bathrooms to the plush purple lobby. It's perhaps not for the strict minimalist, but the decadent Panache Penthouse comes equipped with decks and is a great party pad; the JG La Vie Balcony Suite (above) might adopt a more neutral palette but is no less lavish, fitted with a bespoke Savoir bed. The hotel also has an exhibition space, curated by a roll call of local galleries and studios. However, by far the best thing about Cachet must be its highly desirable address – a lovely 1920s art deco building located bang in the middle of Jing'an.
931 Nanjing Xilu (entrance on Taixing Lu), T 6217 9000, www.cachethotels.com

Urbn

Indisputably one of the top design hotels in Shanghai, this boutique property was also given a facelift by the Cachet Group (opposite) after acquiring it in 2014. A leafy courtyard with a terrace tucked back from the street leads to the reclaimed-timber lobby – the place is an urban oasis in the cluttered Jing'an district. The renovated rooms, such as the Garden View (above), feature lacquered wood, tatami-inspired bed frames and subdued tones. Urbn proudly pitches itself as a carbon-neutral hotel – it sources eco-friendly suppliers, uses recycled and indigenous materials, and buys carbon credits to offset guests' footprints. Rooms have been fitted with a custom-built air purification system, which combats China's worrying pollution index. *183 Jiaozhou Lu, T 5153 4600, www.urbnhotels.com*

24 HOURS
SEE THE BEST OF THE CITY IN JUST ONE DAY

Shanghai is dense and energetic, so you can get a lot done even on a stopover. But in one of the world's most digitalised cities, make sure you charge up your phone and download the WeChat app. It's used for everything from maps and bookings to hailing a ride and instant payments, even at street stalls. Start the day drinking in the views from a Pudong hotel (see p016). Cross over to The Bund for photo ops looking back to the Oriental Pearl (1 Century Avenue) et al. Around here, many art deco buildings have been restored, including the Rockbund Art Museum (see p027) and the Fairmont Peace Hotel (see p072), one of the first skyscrapers in the East.

Next, head to People's Park, the old British race club reclaimed by the PRC in 1952. The Museum of Contemporary Art (231 Nanjing Xilu, T 6327 9900) is a former greenhouse reworked by Atelier Liu Yuyang, although its exhibitions do tend towards the commercial. More interesting is the Urban Planning Exhibition Center (100 Renmin Dadao, T 6318 4477), which charts Shanghai's relentless assault on the sky in a huge model. Then take a trip to the West Bund's museums (see p028) or explore the quirky boutiques (see p080), bars and markets in the lanes of the French Concession, in particular Taikang Lu's antiques stalls, Tianzifang (see p072), Julu Lu for its eateries and lively Dongping Lu. End with a refined meal at Fu He Hui (see p030) or under the stars at Calypso (see p037). *For full addresses, see Resources.*

09.00 Farine

Franck Pecol's eponymous bistro (T 6437 6465) opened in 2007 and proved a hit for its quality ingredients, often imported. In 2012, the French restaurateur followed up with this organic artisan bakery next door, and there are now three further branches. Farine means 'flour', and bread, pastries and cakes are baked on site; the almond croissants are legendary. Neri&Hu's warm fit-out melds reclaimed elm, blackened bronze, raw concrete and white tiles. In warm weather, head out to the communal table to people-watch – pretty Wukang Lu is popular with fashion bloggers taking street shots. Afterwards, browse the shops and galleries in Ferguson Lane (No 376). If you'd prefer a Chinese breakfast, order *jianbing* (egg crepe) and *cifangao* (sticky rice cake) from the stalls on Xiangyang Lu. *378 Wukang Lu, www.farine-bakery.com*

10.30 Shanghai Sculpture Space

Located in the Red Town arts village at the west end of the city, this cavernous 2,500 sq m space, which opened in 2005, displays sculptures and installations by some of China's best-known artists in the converted interiors of a 1950s steel plant. The project signalled a pragmatic new alliance between cutting-edge creatives and Shanghai's property developers. The sculpture garden in the surrounding park is also a draw, thanks to its wide lawn and rotating roster of works. Visit mid-morning to give yourself some time to stroll around the large site. The other galleries in Red Town are more contrived, but the complex itself, with its industrial architecture and quiet cafés, provides an airy and pleasant escape from the daytime crowds outside. *570 Huaihai Xilu, T 6280 7844, www.sss570.com*

13.00 Rockbund Art Museum

This 1923 art deco building has long been a marker of Shanghai's cultural heritage. It was formerly the HQ of the Royal Asiatic Society and, since 2010, when it received a facelift by David Chipperfield as part of a regeneration of 11 iconic buildings on the North Bund, has been home to arguably the city's most tenured and well-respected contemporary art museum. In comparison with the many private ventures that have cropped up in newly created arts districts like Red Town (opposite), the Rockbund is a veteran with real street cred that shows some of the most renowned Chinese artists of recent decades, including Cai Guo-Qiang and Zeng Fanzhi. It is known for its new-media savvy too: download the WeChat app to get a guide sent to you as you peruse. *20 Huqiu Lu, T 3310 9985, www.rockbundartmuseum.org*

15.00 Long Museum West Bund

Designed by Atelier Deshaus and opened in 2014, this concrete monolith beside the Huangpu is characterised by a jigsaw of mushroom-shaped vaulted columns built around the remains of a standalone 1950s coal-ferry unloading bridge. Each forms a wall and ceiling plane, creating a series of cantilevered overhangs filled in with glass, often shielded from the sun by perforated metal. It is hugely atmospheric. The Long's collection, acquired by the billionaire Liu Yiqian, includes both contemporary work, by the likes of 'scar artist' He Duoling and 'cynical realist' Fang Lijun, across the upper floors (opposite), and ancient Chinese art and artefacts (basement). The restaurant has river views and is a nice spot for lunch; the Yuz Museum (see p058) is next door. *3398 Longteng Dadao, T 6422 7636, www.thelongmuseum.org*

Fu He Hui

Chinese vegetarianism has its roots Buddhism, and Tony Lu has evoked a zen vibe at Michelin-starred Fu He Hui, from the understated design, delicate carvings and art to such indigenous ingredients as taro, white sesame, lily bulbs, kai-lan, longan and lotus seeds. Along with the five regular tables, 11 private rooms offer total immersion. *1037 Yuyuan Lu, T 3980 9188*

d nightlife scene is volatile and flighty – bars and
pen, close or morph into a totally different entity
from one week to the next. And in a city as big and chaotic as this,
hundreds of events happen on the same date, so it's not unusual
for an evening to have four or five stops, as clued-up hipsters hop
from supper to gallery to party to late-night karaoke session.

Flash Unico (2nd floor, Three on the Bund, 3 Zhongshan Dong
Yi Lu, T 5308 5399), which has a Latin flavour, and Bar Rouge (7th
floor, 18 Zhongshan Dong Yi Lu, T 6339 1199), all bottle service and
go-go dancers, cater for exhibitionists – something that Shanghai
does well. There's a hipper attitude at music-conscious haunts Craft
(see p044) and Arcade (2nd floor, 57 Fuxing Xilu, T 1670 0335). If
you're more interested in the actual drinks, Speak Low (579 Fuxing
Zhonglu, T 6416 0133), a speakeasy with a hidden entrance, and
whisky bar Lab (1093 Wuding Lu, T 6255 1195) are top-notch.

The Bund is known for European ventures run by super-chefs,
from Jean-Georges (Three on the Bund, 3 Zhongshan Dong Yi Lu,
T 6321 7733) to Maison Pourcel (35 Shanxi Nanlu, T 6215 8777). But
you must dine on Chinese cuisine too. Seek out the charming Old
Jesse (41 Tianping Lu, T 6282 9260), Lost Heaven (17 Yan'an Donglu,
T 6330 0967), for Yunnan dishes, and try the *shengjianbao* (pork
dumplings) at Xiao Yang's stall (269 Wujiang Lu, T 6136 1391).
For full addresses, see Resources.

Baoism

Self-styled 'modern street food' specialist Baoism updates the *guabao*, a steamed clamshell-shaped bun stuffed with meat, often roast pork. The imaginative fillings include pepper tofu, carnitas, and Korean fried chicken, accompanied by sides such as lotus chips and Japanese-style onsen egg (slow-cooked in warm water). Local studio Linehouse drew inspiration from the bamboo steamer for the interiors, using perforated metal panels to separate the dining area from the kitchen; and the custom high stools reference the small seats clustered on street corners in China. BaoBao (380 Shanxi Nanlu) is a similar concept that specialises in closed-top *bao*. From the street stalls, keep an eye out for Shanghai classics *shengjianbao* (opposite) and *congyoubing* (green-onion pancakes). *150 Hubin Lu B2/E30, T 6333 5676*

Green & Safe

This polished organic deli and eaterie is
Shanghai's answer to Whole Foods, and
then some, as all the local produce and
meat comes from the company farm in
Kunshan, just outside the city. E-commerce
grocers and delivery services had already
started to take off here, and this is the first
iteration of the concept as a physical store
and restaurant rolled into one. The canteen
(right) serves a simple, seasonal menu;
drop by for a Thai basil salad with minced
beef and chilli, or pressed beetroot and
carrot juice. The upstairs Asian-Western
fusion restaurant, Green Kitchen, occupies
a loft-style space under a trussed timber
roof, with communal tables and lounge-
style seating. Most dishes come as small
sharing plates; highly recommended are
the stout-braised pork chops with stir-
fried vegetables, 10-hour sous vide beef,
and spaghetti served with whole lobster.
6 Dongping Lu, T 5465 1288,
www.green-n-safe.com

Seesaw Coffee

Start your day right with a speciality brew from this artisan coffee shop, a favourite of stylish insiders since opening in 2012 within the Jing'an Design Center, a small compound of creative workspaces. The café is airy and bright, especially if you can find a seat among the potted plants on the monochrome-tiled patio, which sits under a glass roof. Seesaw's baristas treat the humble bean with reverence, and roasting is performed in-house. For your brew, choose from siphon, hand-drip or espresso. Sample something local and a little different, perhaps the single-origin, small-batch blend from Yunnan (a region that is better known for its tea), paired with a treat from Strictly Cookies (T 137 8894 0337), which has a deserved cult following. *433 Yuyuan Lu, T 5204 7828, www.seesawcoffee.com*

Calypso

Shigeru Ban's house of bamboo and glass is a breath of fresh air amid the high-rises and air-con malls of Jing'an. The architect collaborated with design firm AvroKO, but Ban's signature turns up subtly throughout, seen in the basket-weave roof panels and the recycled paper used as ornamentation. When the weather permits, the glass walls of the ground floor slide up to the ceiling, and upstairs in the lounge, the roof recedes for an alfresco ambience. Alvaro Roa's Mediterranean cuisine visits Spain, Italy and the south of France in dishes such as Galician-style Atlantic octopus, Iberico pork chops marinated in paprika, and house-made linguine with lobster. Just about every reputable food blogger has drooled over the stone-baked pizza.
Kerry Centre Piazza, Tongren Lu/An Yi Lu, T 2203 8888

Liquid Laundry

Restaurateur Kelley Lee is already behind the wildly popular Boxing Cat Brewery (T 6431 2091) and Cantina Agave (T 6886 0706), a taquería that introduced casual US-Mexican-style dining to Shanghai. In a similar vein, Liquid Laundry dishes up American soul food, and has been a huge hit since opening in 2014. From the open kitchen arrives upmarket bar fare made with quality ingredients, from pizza topped with Merguez sausage, onion jam and feta, to beer-braised beef-tongue sliders, truffle fries and duck nuggets. The loft-inspired space seats 200 on mismatched furniture, and a neon-lit bar offers draft beers brewed on site, bourbons and craft cocktails. The see-and-be-seen mood is amplified when DJs play. Book well ahead. *KWah Centre, 1028 Huaihai Zhonglu, T 6445 9589, www.theliquidlaundry.com*

Le Baron

André Saraiva's Shanghai venture is similar in atmosphere and concept to its sister outposts in Paris, London, New York and Tokyo. Storeage Amsterdam has given it an old-time peep-show vibe, with leather doors, brass-trimmed marble tabletops, semi-transparent mirrors and bordello-style lighting. It's a little heavy-handed with the velvet but the effect is moody and intimate. The motif covering the carpets and wallpaper is created from a sketch drawn by Saraiva, and lends the space a racy intensity. Le Baron hosts parties for the likes of Kitsune and Prada, meaning the crowd is an edgy mix of jet-setting bright young things and local scenesters. Beats range from hip hop to trippy electro, with Parisian DJ Victor Aime at the helm. *7th floor, 20 Donghu Lu, T 6483 2061, www.lebaronshanghai.com*

The Nest

Since opening in 2014, this lounge bar has been a hot destination for a smart crowd of media execs who eschew The Bund's flashier rooftop bars exemplified by the 24th-floor M1NT (T 6391 3191), with its 17m-long shark tank. It fills up after 9pm, but, despite its address, has an unpretentious atmosphere. A coiling colour-shifting light sculpture is a showpiece over the bar, and clusters of armchairs create an intimate tone. The high-quality cocktails are mostly vodka-based; a Cinnamon Pear Sour, for example, mixes Grey Goose, Poire William, syrup and lime. Well suited is a Nordic-inspired menu that focuses on raw and seafood dishes, including Fine de Claire oysters served with mini syringes of ginger ponzu, and rye bread toast topped with Arctic shrimp in a creamy dill sauce.
6th floor, 130 Beijing Donglu, T 6308 7669

Coquille

Next to John Liu's wildly popular Italian trattoria Scarpetta (T 3376 8223), this two-storey Gallic seafood spot, loosely modelled on a French Concession villa, is another hit. Alongside the signature platter, a towering shrine to shellfish, locals come for the Dungeness crab with spices, and escargot with lemongrass-ginger butter and aromatic kaffir lime.
29-31 Mengzi Lu, T 3376 8127

Craft

Tucked down a nondescript alleyway and hidden on top of a teppanyaki joint, this 'secret' hipster bar is the unofficial vodka specialist of Shanghai, offering an array of craft batches from all around the world; cocktails feature fragrant house infusions made using ingredients including Chinese tea, flowers and fruit. But Craft is perhaps better known for progressive music, as DJs use the decks to test out new tracks on a savvy crowd. Stripped-back concrete, steel and reclaimed teak give the elongated bar a dressed-up industrial edge; the grey walls showcase the work of local photographers and artists. A more intimate area out back is fitted with sofas and a chandelier made from plastic-tube lighting. Come after 11pm on a Thursday or Friday – if you can find it. *2nd floor, 7 Donghu Lu, Donghu Hotel South Wing, T 6418 9338*

The Commune Social

Chef Jason Atherton and design studio Neri&Hu first partnered at Waterhouse's (see p018) Table No 1, a sleek, subdued hotel restaurant. This follow-up is buzzier, and flush with creative types. The interiors have an industrial feel, but if the weather's fine, nab a table in the lovely courtyard for Atherton's modern Spanish tapas (he was the first Brit to work at ElBulli), from scallop ceviche with avocado, jalapeno jelly and pear, to warm sea urchin with pepper butter served on ciabatta. It's the first stage in a 'moveable feast' concept: afterwards, head to the dessert counter, where the pastry chefs prepare European and Asian treats to order. Finish in the moody cocktail bar with the Jing'an Juice, a mix of gin, pineapple, basil and ginger. *511 Jiangning Lu, T 6047 7638, www.communesocial.com*

Xibo

This is a stylish alternative to the usually flamboyant Xinjiang dining style, where regional music and dance performances are de rigueur. Xibo serves north-western fare in a refreshingly chic setting; yet the menu itself is superbly authentic, with Uighur standards – lamb, beef, spices and flatbreads – and dishes influenced by neighbouring Kazakhstan and Russia.
3rd floor, 83 Changshu Lu, T 5403 8330

Chi Q

Husband-and-wife duo Jean-Georges and Marja Vongerichten's Chi Q shares all the style and dim lighting of many high-end Bund dining spots, but the menu – with its reworking of Marja's Korean family recipes, a spin-off from her TV series the *Kimchi Chronicles* – sets it apart. Signature dishes, including bibimbap topped with foie gras, are rich and playful. Neri&Hu's interiors are more adventurous than their usual MO here: the walls are clad in charred wood panels and the slender rafters evoke a bamboo forest. At the restaurant's heart is a communal table situated beneath a soaring quadruple-height ceiling, lit by supersized pendant bulbs, while half-sunken banquettes fringe tables fitted with grills for BBQing the Wagyu beef.
Three on the Bund, 3 Zhongshan Dong Yi Lu, T 6321 6622, www.threeonthebund.com

Mr & Mrs Bund

Chef Paul Pairet launched The Bund's first 'after-hours' restaurant in 2009. Billed as a 'modern French eaterie', the style here is relaxed; dishes are created to be shared, and staff dress in jeans and sneakers. A 250-item menu covers the classics such as boeuf bourguignon, and more interesting dishes, including crispy duck leg confit with roasted ceps and seared foie gras, while the lemon tart, which takes 72 hours to prepare and is presented as if it were the fruit itself, is legendary. A 2015 facelift by Kokaistudios gave the interiors a more elegant look, with a deep blue, beige and slate palette, chevron wood floors, custom Murano chandeliers and trompe l'oeil wall panelling. Meanwhile, the glowing view of Pudong's skyline remains a major draw. *6th floor, 18 Zhongshan Dong Yi Lu, T 6323 9898, www.mmbund.com*

Yè Shanghai

Authentic, traditional Shanghainese food is hard to come by these days, as migration from across China means most restaurants offer cuisine from the various regions. Yè Shanghai, a clever, inventive renovation of a Xintiandi lanehouse, keeps it old school by channelling a 1920s feel and specialising in classic dishes such as *xiaolongbao* (juicy pork dumplings, which are prepared in a bamboo steamer), slow-braised pak choi and 'lion's head' meatballs (so-called due to their majestic size). The name means Shanghai Nights, but this is definitely a better bet for lunch. The smaller room on the upper floor, which can be booked for private dining, has views across the tiled roofs. We suggest hosting your farewell lunch here before hotfooting it out of town. *338 Huangpi Nanlu, T 6311 2323, www.elite-concepts.com*

Taste

Launched in 2013 by photographer Viko Wu and designer Yutaka Onozawa, Taste purveys stylish lifestyle and homewares products – from fragrances by Mad et Len to glassware by Seikosha Studio and Haws watering cans – and moved to Tianzifang two years later to add a café/restaurant and exhibition area to the mix. As with the wares, the emphasis is on craftsmanship. Espresso and hand-drip coffee, which is often served by Yutaka, are offered in a chic space, fitted with custom furniture, with attention to detail extending to menus on paper handmade by the staff. The light lunch options, from salmon carpaccio to a green salad served with Yunnan ham and an onsen egg, change seasonally. Do not skip the matcha red bean millefeuille.
Building 3, No 105, Lane 210, Taikang Lu, T 2104 1418

INSIDER'S GUIDE

STEVEN OO, FASHION DESIGNER

Chinese-Burmese-US knitwear designer Steven Oo founded the womenswear label One Grey Day (www.onegreyday.com) and has a background as cosmopolitan as his adopted city. 'Shanghai is the place to be as it is a mix of many different influences,' he says. Oo likes to visit the Ming Contemporary Art Museum (436 Yonghe Donglu, T 6445 1199), where installations frequently involve live performance, and Lafayette Arts & Design Centre (323 Fuxing Zhonglu), housed in László Hudec's (see p077) art deco cinema. His favourite shops are Dong Liang (see p092) – 'If you can't make Fashion Week, just head here' – multi-brand Mianhuatian (564 Changle Lu, T 5403 5103), mainly for its imaginative displays inside a restored Concession-era villa, and Wondullful Dept (2nd floor, 1728 Nanjing Xilu, T 5466 6337), for quirky homewares. To unwind, he heads to the PuLi's Anantara Spa (see p016) for a massage.

At weekends, he will meet friends for brunch at U Gastronomy (368 Wukang Lu, T 5435 5737), a European restaurant located in a 1920s mansion, and in the evenings, he enjoys Fu He Hui (see p030) for its calm aura. Hakkasan (5th floor, Bund 18, 18 Zhongshan Dong Yi Lu, T 6321 5888) is another favourite due to its views and quality Cantonese cuisine: 'I love the ambience and classic presentation.' If it's to be a late night, he will head to Lab (see p032) or The Nest (see p041). And after hours, there's always Le Baron (see p040). *For full addresses, see Resources.*

ART AND DESIGN
GALLERIES, STUDIOS AND PUBLIC SPACES

There has been a calculated effort to turn Shanghai into mainland China's soft power base as the government recognises its value to the economy, and the influx of huge institutions has been referred to as a 'museumification' of the city. The state-run Power Station of Art (see p064) and China Art Museum (World Expo Park, 205 Shangnan Lu, T 400 921 9021) launched in 2012, and partner with Western bodies to put on headline shows. Then two billionaires opened the Long Museum (see p028) and Yuz Museum (see p058), competing to outdo each other in cavernous halls. They have since been joined by the West Bund Art Center (2555 Longteng Dadao), ShanghART (see p067) and SCoP (see p068) to form a cluster of venues in a post-industrial landscape. Other independent galleries are flourishing too. Pearl Lam (181 Jiangxi Zhonglu, T 6323 1989) represents some of the top names in the country, and many quality establishments are found in the M50 arts district (see p063).

The growth of the design scene has been a tad more organic. Shanghai International Creative Industry Week began in 2005, soon bolstered by Design Shanghai, and there is no lack of grass roots creativity. Ateliers to watch include Zhang Zhoujie Digital Lab (see p060), MVW (see p066) and Benwu Studio (Suite 1401, Building 2, 1728 Huangxing Lu, Yangpu, T 136 4620 5249). Design Republic Commune (see p070) is where everyone comes together. *For full addresses, see Resources.*

LIFE / DEATH

Tang Shipeng

Graphic design in Shanghai had a heyday in the 1920s and 1930s with the rise of the publishing industry and developments in mass communication. Creative cover art for books and magazines, predominantly in woodblock prints and lithography, was a rich cultural trend; Lu Xun was one of the prominent figures. The style was a uniquely Chinese aesthetic that took influences from art nouveau, art deco, Soviet suprematism and constructivism, and native bronze and stone carvings. These days, Shanghai is the nexus of the country's fledgling advertising industry, and the output of many studios reflects the commercial zeitgeist. However, local Tang Shipeng (*Life and Death*, above, ¥200) is part of a new breed of graphic designers to have reintroduced a fine-art touch. Purchase prints via his website. *www.designtang.com*

Yuz Museum

Chinese-Indonesian billionaire Budi Tek's Yuz Foundation is devoted to promoting contemporary art in the developing world. This 2014 venture, in a pair of converted aircraft hangars on the regenerated West Bund strip dubbed the Cultural Corridor, is its most ambitious to date. Independently curated, the vast space houses more than 1,000 works generously laid out, including 100 from Tek's own hoard. The collector is renowned for his penchant for oversized installations and ambitious undertakings: the 2016 Alberto Giacometti retrospective (right) brought together 250 pieces. The building was converted by Sou Fujimoto, who called it a 'green cube' (as opposed to the traditional white). A soaring glass-box atrium supported on huge pillars leads to the sheds, which are painted vivid red.
35 Fenggu Lu, T 6426 1901,
www.yuzmshanghai.org

Zhang Zhoujie Digital Lab

One of Shanghai's most visionary talents, Zhang Zhoujie has been globally lauded for his limited-edition furniture and objets d'art. Zhoujie has developed a fabrication method in which designs are generated by algorithms on a computer, followed by an assembly procedure that features laser-cutting, and then joining and polishing by hand – effectively inverting the usual model. His '#6141' chair, a multi-faceted metallic throne, sold out in 10 minutes at 100% Design London in 2011; we love the elegant ripple-effect stainless-steel '#SQN1-M' bench (above). To commission a bespoke piece or buy direct, arrange an appointment to visit his studio (opposite) in Songjiang. His gleaming, otherworldly creations are stacked to the ceiling. *Building 205, Block 24, 2908 Renmin Beilu, T 3771 7551, www.zhangzhoujie.com*

SPSI Art Museum

Founded back in 1965, the Oil Painting and Sculpture Institute was the main authority in town before the rise of Shanghai's new wave of conceptual gallerists and artists. Chen Yifei, who was a prominent figure in the development of Chinese painting (he is best known in the West for his romantic realist depiction of women in traditional dress playing instruments), was a member, as well as other big guns. In 2010, the SPSI unveiled this public museum in a stocky polygon of concrete blocks designed by architect Wang Yan. It provides a pleasing juxtaposition with the surrounding glass offices, and a visit makes for a tranquil experience as it is nicely atmospheric within. It predominantly puts on group shows or retrospectives of 20th-century Chinese artists. Closed Mondays.
111 Jinzhu Lu, T 6275 9930

Vanguard Gallery

Since 2004, Vanguard has been fostering and promoting young Asian artists, with an emphasis on photography, video and new media but also encompassing performance art and more traditional disciplines. The group show 'Warehouse Story IV' (above) featured work by Xiao Jiang, Zhang Lehua, Hsu Che-yu, Liu Fei and Gao Mingyan. Its ongoing Gas Station project invites totally undiscovered artists to exhibit, turning it into an experimental platform. Vanguard was one of the first tenants to move in to the M50 arts district, which used to be well signposted by the 'Great Wall of Graffiti', a rare 'uncensored' canvas for street art in this city. But it is under threat of demolition as developers rub their hands (one stretch has already gone) – catch it while you can. *R204, Building 4a, 50 Moganshan Lu, T 5252 2551, www.vanguardgallery.com*

Power Station of Art

The massive Nanshi Power Plant, built in 1985, has undergone two transformations at the hands of Chinese architects Original Design Studio: first into a hall for the 2010 World Expo and later on into this immense museum. The conversion preserved its spatial order and industrial characteristics to create a multi-path experience through seven storeys that even incorporates the inside of the 165m chimney. As the first public museum in China to focus solely on contemporary art, the PSA caused a stir on inauguration in 2012, but its debut as the host of the 9th Shanghai Biennale was criticised for hasty, careless production, including typos in the labels. By the 11th Biennale in 2016, however, it had well and truly found its footing. Closed Mondays.
200 Huayuangang Lu, T 3110 8550,
www.powerstationofart.com

Design MVW

This independent interiors and furniture studio launched in 2005 and has become one of the mainstays of the design realm, having built up a mantelpiece of awards and a hefty portfolio – the Shanghai Tang flagship store at Cathay Mansions is their handiwork. Founded by Franco-Chinese couple Xu Ming, a designer, and Virginie Moriette, an architect, MVW's elegant pieces are hewn from distinctive woods such as dark-lacquered oak and wenge that provide a lush, contemporary take on a classic aesthetic. The 'Yang' vanity cabinet (above) was part of a collaboration with the Italian brand Giorgetti. Crafted from Canaletto walnut, seven sleek drawers are crowned by a circular mirror that appears to float within its sleek rectangular frame. *322 Xingguo Lu, T 6281 5594, www.design-mvw.com*

ShanghART West Bund

Established in 1996 by Swiss-born dealer
Lorenz Helbling, ShanghART is one of the
stalwarts of the contemporary scene and
was the first Chinese gallery to participate
in the international fairs. What began as a
small operation on a few corridor walls at
The Portman Ritz-Carlton has grown into
a highly active and reputable organisation
that represents many of Shanghai's more
influential, if not always groundbreaking
artists. After a long tenure in a couple of
warehouses in the M50 district (see p063),
it celebrated its 20th anniversary with an
expansion to the West Bund and a flagship
that evokes the area's history, resembling
a stack of shipping containers. The second
show, 'Holzewege', featured pieces by Zhao
Yang and Zhang Qing (left to right, above).
2555-10 Longteng Dadao, T 6359 3923,
www.shanghartgallery.com

Shanghai Centre of Photography

Run by Pulitzer Prize winner Liu Heung Shing, China's first museum dedicated to photography is another tick for the West Bund. The concrete-and-glass structure, an ensemble of elliptical volumes, was designed by Johnston Marklee as a pavilion for the 2013 biennale, and repurposed in 2015. An enclosed atrium and skylights provide illumination, and circulation is meandering. Exhibitions often spotlight Chinese artists – 'Grain to Pixel' explored the evolution of photography, from the pioneering Lang Jingshan to propaganda shots by Chairman Mao's documentarian Wu Yinxian, and Lu Nan's black-and-white stories. 'Nature: A Subjective Place' (above) featured the US artist Harry Callahan and locals Lin Ran, Ni Youyu and Luo Yongjin. *2555-1 Longteng Dadao, T 6428 9516, www.scop.org.cn*

K11 Art Space

This vast display floor in the basement of a mall is a cornerstone of Hong Kong's K11 Foundation's mission to raise the profile of contemporary art in hyper-consumerist China. Launched in 2013, the self-styled 'art playground' is all about accessibility, through workshops, talks, competitions and a wide spectrum of exhibitions, from shows by up-and-coming native talent to retrospectives on Dalí and Monet. The collection, which is also integrated into the retail area, includes pieces by Chinese artists, such as *Trace 1* by Liu Jianhua, a large-scale porcelain sculpture that evokes calligraphy, made using a blowtorch. The complex was designed by Shanghai-based Kokaistudios, who installed a mirrored kaleidoscope for a reception desk (above). *300 Huaihai Zhonglu, T 2310 3188, www.k11.com/corp/art*

Design Republic Commune

When the architects Lyndon Neri and Rossana Hu acquired this old Shanghai police station, an early 20th-century brick building, they set about renovating it with a mix of visually lighter materials, including metal sheets and white plaster. In particular, the generous use of glass panels has opened up the corridors and various levels, offsetting the heaviness of the original structure. It launched in 2012 as a showroom for Neri&Hu's range of furniture, lighting and homewares, as well as more than 80 other high-profile global interiors and lifestyle brands. It acts as a clubhouse for the local design community; there's a gallery and events space for talks and exhibitions, and an adjoining restaurant and bar (see p045). *511 Jiangning Lu, T 6176 7088, www.thedesignrepublic.com*

ARCHITOUR

A GUIDE TO SHANGHAI'S ICONIC BUILDINGS

The supercharged rate of urban development in today's China has created a cityscape shaped more like great piles of money than anything else. Look out over Shanghai's skyline and you may make out as many construction cranes as buildings. An ever-inflating property bubble sees developers breaking ground at a pace that would be unimaginable anywhere else, and large international architecture firms are vying for their piece of the pie. The rapidly multiplying cluster of towers in Pudong (see p012), plus Shimao International Plaza (819 Nanjing Donglu) and Tomorrow Square (see p013) flanking People's Park, tell the post-millennial story.

The city's 20th-century heritage lies in its art deco structures, pioneered by architects including László Hudec (see p077), and its swathes of *longtang* – rows of grey brick houses, the equivalent of European terraces, which form maze-like passageways – that were once the definitive hallmark of the city, but now dwindle by the day as the bulldozers clear more and more space. The restored buildings found in the Rockbund area are a good introduction to Shanghai deco, as are the Guotai Cinema (870 Huaihai Zhonglu) and The Bund promenade's Fairmont Peace Hotel (20 Nanjing Donglu, T 6138 6888). Also check out the restoration of Tianzifang in the French Concession, where an entire *longtang* district has been repurposed into a mini-village of studios, shops and cafés. *For full addresses, see Resources.*

Poly Grand Theatre

Shanghai's exponential growth has seen the birth of satellite communities in rapidly sprawling 'burbs. In an attempt to establish local hubs among the soulless condos and malls, 'landmark' cultural centres are being built, of which Tadao Ando's theatre is the most successful. It opened in 2014 on an artificial lake in Jiading, 20km north-west of the centre, and is a Froebelian fantasy. Five steel cylinders dissect a concrete box faced in aluminium and glass. They are arranged horizontally, vertically (to form a six-storey atrium) and diagonally, which creates elliptical openings that function as terraces and semi-outdoor amphitheatres at ground level and on the roof. One tube connects to a hotel, office and retail tower (above, behind), also by Ando. The theatre itself seats 1,600 and has fine acoustics.
159 Baiyin Lu, T 5951 3377

Natural History Museum
Perkins+Will took the nautilus shell as
inspiration for this 2015 eco-friendly
museum. It spirals down six levels from
the parkland roof of its living facade
(pictured) to enclose a 30m-high glass
lobby, and an interior cell-like structure
of white lattice around a central pond
and cascading terraces in the style of
a Chinese mountain and water garden.
510 Beijing Lu, T 6862 2000

1933

This former abattoir is one of the most dramatic and idiosyncratic buildings in Shanghai. Named after its completion date and designed by British architects, it is in essence an ornate concrete shell. Behind a huge, imposing screen carved with art deco details, the cavernous and low-slung spaces, bridges and curving staircases create an eerie, Escher-esque interior. A 2008 restoration, led by Paul Liu, former director of Three on the Bund (see p049), and architect Zhao Chongxin, aimed to transform it into a creative and commercial hub; it now houses an event space, restaurants and a clutch of stores, though the ambition of the project is still unrealised. Luckily, the overhaul has not detracted from the haunting ambience.

611 Liyang Lu, Hongkou, T 6888 1933,
www.1933shanghai.com

Christian Literature Society Building

Hungarian-Slovak architect László Hudec escaped the Russians en route to a gulag in Siberia in 1916, crossed into China and ended up in Shanghai, becoming one of its most notable exponents of art deco. His output included the 1933 Grand Theatre (216 Nanjing Xilu) and the nearby 1934 Park Hotel (170 Nanjing Xilu), the city's tallest building for half a century. The lesser-known Christian Literature Society Building, from 1932, incorporates strong perpendicular lines in red and black brick, and neo-Gothic and German expressionist elements in the flowering finials of its pilasters. The institution was the first to introduce Western texts to the country; these days the block sits eerily vacant. Opposite is Hudec's 1934 headquarters for the China Baptist Publication Society. *128 Huqiu Lu*

Oriental Sports Center

In the lightning-quick manner of Chinese state building projects, the construction of this mammoth ¥2bn complex, drawn up by GMP, was completed in 30 months, from bid to opening ceremony, for the 2011 FINA World Championships. It consists of three structures: a multi-use stadium hall, a natatorium with four pools, and a media centre, and uses 3,000 tons of steel. The design features broad arches with curved surfaces, as well as triangular elements that evoke sails. In keeping with recent urban planning policies, it is a sustainable development, and perches on a manmade lake in former industrial brownfield land. Pudong New Area is also home to the 2010 Expo Park, a huge undertaking that has since become something of a ghost town.
300 Yongyao Lu, T 2023 2008,
www.orientalsportscenter.cn

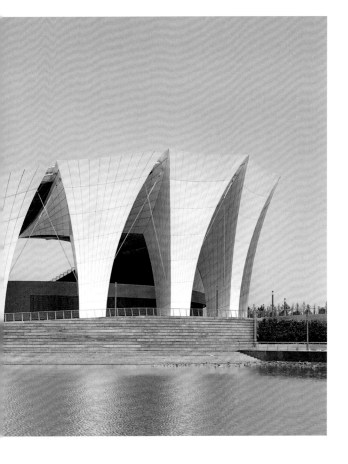

SHOPS

THE BEST RETAIL THERAPY AND WHAT TO BUY

The Chinese market has been aggressively courted in recent years by the top global fashion houses, which advertise heavily and open multiple locations in the city's many high-end malls, meaning that the local industry struggles to carve out space. Concept stores such as Triple-Major (see p085) and Dong Liang Studio (see p092) are fighting back by carrying emerging Chinese brands alongside hip international labels. There is also a growing number of designers whose showrooms can be visited by appointment. Among the best are Nicole Zhang (see p090), Qiu Hao (info@qiuhaoqiuhao.com), Masha Ma (info@masha-ma.com) and Uma Wang (T 6262 2032).

For more of an earthy flavour, the little stores on Nanchang Lu and Julu Lu are fun to browse, and the haberdashery and fabric market in South Bund (399 Lujiabang Lu) is perfect for something bespoke – a unique part of the China experience. Sneakerheads should check out Culture Matters (206 Wulumuqi Zhonglu, T 136 7188 2040) for vintage kicks, including Feiyue and Warrior. Annabel Lee (No 1, Lane 8, Zhongshan Dong Yi Lu, T 6445 8218) is the place for embroidered silks with a contemporary touch. The traditional *qipao*, or *cheongsam*, can also make a striking memento. The tailor who created Maggie Cheung's dresses in the Cantonese film *In The Mood For Love* is a true homegrown treasure, and has a shop in the French Concession, Hanyi (217 Changle Lu, T 5404 2303).
For full addresses, see Resources.

Alter

In the last decade, high-end fashion here has been dominated by flashy logos and big brands, but tastes are slowly starting to shift. At this cutting-edge store, Sonja Xiao Long is bringing alternative Western designers such as JW Anderson, Anthony Vaccarello and Jonathan Saunders to Chinese shoppers, often for the first time, as well as a great roster of hard-to-find Japanese and Korean labels like Yohanix and Facetasm. Its in-house brand, Rolling Acid, has built up a cult following for its bold graphics and streetwear-inspired silhouettes. The edgy, warehouse-esque interior, which was revamped in 2015, is distinguished by a series of bamboo-crate display units. Grab a drink or snack as you browse from the Alter Cube coffee counter. *Shop L116, Xintiandi Style, 245 Madang Lu, T 6302 9889, www.alterstyle.com*

Banmoo

Meaning 'half wood' in Chinese, Banmoo is the project of local designer Lv Yongzhong. Since opening a small Xintiandi storefront in 2006, Banmoo set up shop in a loft-like Changing location, before making the leap to this multi-level space, styled as a home, and well-suited to displaying its sculptural furniture. The 'Calligraphy' chair resembles a Chinese character and is fashioned from laser-cut ribs of fibreboard, exemplifying the brand's melding of technology and cultural history, as does the 'Long' table, which is inspired by the *guqin*, a zither-like instrument, with a profile that evokes Han dynasty costumes. We are also fans of the smaller items, particularly the rosewood boxes for storing books, and the 'Carrying Moon' incense holder (above), ¥420.
Room B122, 258 Wending Lu, T 6128 5818, www.banmoo.cn

Coterie

Until Coterie set up shop in 2012, Chinese opticians were huge chains with a clinical, rather than fashionable, feel. The Xintiandi flagship boutique has a monochrome fit-out, marble tabletops, mosaic floors and full-length mirrors to encourage customers to find a pair of specs that not only suits their face, but also their whole look. It sells chic, high-end frames and sunglasses by brands such as Prism, Henry Holland, LGR and Chrome Hearts, as well as globally sourced vintage pieces – ask to see the pre-owned stash of retro Dior, Persol and more. Coterie commissions international creatives, including typography artist Pieter Ceizer and illustrator Casper Chan, to create its window treatments, and its lookbooks are directed by Chen Man, who has exhibited at MOCA (see p024).

L104 South Block, www.coterie.cn

SPRING/SUMMER NEW ARRIVALS

Triple-Major

Shanghai's last word in up-and-coming fashion labels, as well as art and design 'zines, Triple-Major occupies four floors within an old townhouse. Local firm Last Design have fronted it with an unfinished cement facade and added fun touches: an oversized inkstone, used as a display table; slim transparent shelving; and succulents poking out of holes. International names from Milan (Damir Doma), Berlin (Bless) and Antwerp (Walter Van Beirendonck) brush shoulders with brands from Beijing, and the house's own line combines playful detailing with conventional shapes and styles. Founder Ritchie Chan and team often curate exhibitions hosted in store. Off the tourist path, this spot is not only a real treat but also refreshingly quiet.
25 Shaoxing Lu, T 6445 3945,
www.triple-major.com

Urban Tribe

An earthy lifestyle boutique and teahouse, this quiet oasis on Fuxing Xilu is run by Jasmine Mu and Gao Ping. The pair have travelled to remote regions of the country to study indigenous crafts and discover heritage materials and patterns. Products are predominantly loungewear, jewellery, ceramics and homewares; fabric dyes are chemical-free, using natural ingredients such as indigo and logwood. We liked the line of hand-thrown tableware painted with traditional green-and-white glazes, and the modern interpretations of the 'ci' embroidery techniques of the tribes of south-west China, used here in the clothes, from wide-fit trousers to tunic dresses. From the café, try one of the teas, perhaps the pu'er, to enjoy in the lovely garden. *133 Fuxing Xilu, T 6433 5366, www.urbantribe.cn*

CASHIER

MEASURE TWICE
CUT ONCE

Aegis
This expert curation of gents' fashion,
footwear and accessories includes an
assembly of labels making their debut
in mainland China. Manly memorabilia
(vintage suitcases, radios) and stylish
darkwood floorboards provide a bold
backdrop for the suave collections. The
downstairs coffee bar serves pour over
among a stash of retro arcade games.
1 Taojiang Lu, T 5419 8226

Nicole Zhang

Since launching her womenswear label in 2012, Shanghai resident Nicole Zhang has conceived two androgynous collections a year, often using unorthodox fabrics like metallic-thread knits and over-dyed denim. Her SS17 looks are sporty, streamlined styles in fun, unfussy silhouettes: louche suits, jersey dresses and disco-inspired outerwear. A light-filled, by-appointment showroom opened in 2014, tucked down a laneway – look for her logo painted on a white garage door. Accessories include skinny choker scarves and deconstructed handbags – the slouchy, oversized clutch can be worn either folded, or threaded through with a leather cable strap. Nicole Zhang is also at Wildjam (T 6209 2307), a stylish multi-label boutique in Hongqiao. *No 1, 17 Wulumuqi Zhonglu, T 6236 0331, www.nicolezhang.com*

Young Chinese Blood

Established in 2014 by brother and sister Xing and Jenny-Jing Zhao, this accessories brand began as a collection of hip printed pocket squares made from Suzhou silk (see p096). The design ideas are references to popular culture, and each has its own story. 'Tango', an intricate paisley, is inspired by Wong Kar-wai's film *Happy Together*, a romance that is set in Argentina; 'Fumo' (above, left), an abbreviation of *Futurismo*, features bold geometric forms; and the monochromic 'Gatsby' (above, right), both ¥400, has a natural sheen that nods to the glamour of 1920s New York. The label has since expanded to include menswear, totes and small leather goods. YCB often stages hyped pop-up events around town, or visit the showroom by appointment. *Naked Hub, 1237 Fuxing Zhonglu, T 136 5178 9350, www.youngchineseblood.com*

Dong Liang Studio

The mother of China's fashion emporiums, Dong Liang Studio has been showcasing on-the-rise homegrown designers since 2009. Originally a Beijing start-up, it now has a much larger HQ in the capital, and this impressive three-storey lane house in Shanghai, restored to retain much of its original flavour, with 1930s-style windows, hardwood floors, beamed ceilings and a leafy courtyard. The focus is on directional pieces, rather than easy-to-wear looks, for both sexes. Founders Charles Wang, Nan Lang and Tasha Liu have now established themselves as unofficial brand-makers, and just about every notable independent in the country, including Uma Wang (see p080) and Guo Pei, has had a collection in Dong Liang at some point or another. Our pick of the rising stars are London-based womenswear designer Yifang Wan and the Beijing streetwear brand Sankuanz.
184 Fumin Lu, T 3469 6926,
www.dongliangchina.com

Eco & More

Offering plant-based, cruelty-free lifestyle and household products, Shanghai firm Eco & More is the brainchild of Australian-Chinese Jeni Saeyang and has made waves by raising awareness about the effects of pollution. Since 2012, the brand has grown from an e-commerce website to this bricks-and-mortar store, opened in 2015 in K11 (see p069); a community space that hosts wellness workshops, from aromatherapy to allergy relief. Amid plenty of greenery and cork display counters is a scent bar for essential oils and refill stations for the best-selling products, including the Thai lemongrass-oil handwash. Eco & More aims to provide for every aspect of a toxin-free life, from laundry liquid to soy candles and even yoga mat spray, all made in China.

B/2 K11 Art Mall, 300 Huaihai Zhonglu, T 5238 1903, www.eco-more.com

Song Fang Maison de Thé

In China, tea is both hallowed and taken for granted – tea shops often look way too much like pharmacies – which is why Song Fang is such a gem. On the corner of a busy street in the French Concession, the bijou store is named after the Chinese translation of its French owner's surname, Florence Samson. After working for luxury firms including Veuve Clicquot and Dior, Samson had the idea of creating a *maison de thé*, selling some of the most exquisite leaves grown in China, such as oolong from Wuyi and pu'er from Yunnan, plus French blends, including fragrant *pomme d'amour* (50g packs range from ¥60 to ¥790). Head up to the second or third floor to sip your chosen *cha*. Teapots (from ¥200 to ¥1,500) and brewing wares are also on sale here.
227 Yongjia Lu, T 6433 8283,
www.songfangtea.com

ESCAPES

WHERE TO GO IF YOU WANT TO LEAVE TOWN

A famous Chinese proverb extolls the ethereal natural landscapes of two destinations within arm's reach of Shanghai: 'The sky has heaven, the earth has Suzhou and Hangzhou.' Indeed, West Lake in Hangzhou (opposite) is one of the most sublime landscapes in the country. Stay outside town at the Fuchun Resort (339 Jiangbin Dong Dadao, T 0571 6346 1111), among the tea plantations. Suzhou (see p100), dubbed the 'Venice of the East', also has the gardens of the imperial elite and is renowned for its textiles – visit the No 1 Silk Factory (94 Nanmen Lu, Cang Lang, T 0512 6561 3733) for a tour. Surrounding Suzhou lie the Yangtze water towns, which developed from 2,500 years ago as a network of prosperous villages linked by boat to the cultural capital. Today, Zhouzhuang (see p102) is the headline attraction, Tongli and Nanxun are more authentic, with locals still going about their daily lives, and in Luzhi you will find the singing boatwomen, a precious and little-known tradition.

Further afield, we recommend Moganshan, which is just under three hours by car. A popular retreat in the 1920s and 1930s, the area has made a comeback – media mogul Hung Huang renovated a house here that used to belong to her mother, and the architect-designed Naked Stables (37 Shangxiazhuang Village, Paitou, T 6431 8901) was a stylish addition. The bamboo-forested mountains are a serene setting for BBQs, hikes and communing with nature. *For full addresses, see Resources.*

CAA Folk Art Museum, Hangzhou

Hangzhou's majestic West Lake, flanked by the Baochu and Leifeng pagodas, has been rhapsodised by writers and artists since the Qin dynasty. But there are also manmade pleasures here, including the China Academy of Art (CAA). The Pritzker Prize winner Shu Wang helms its School of Architecture and his studio is behind the majority of its campus buildings. Wang's penchant for recycled materials is seen in the use of more than two million salvaged tiles. The Folk Art Museum, located in an old tea plantation within the grounds, is a 2015 Kengo Kuma project that continues this leitmotif with a series of zigzagging pitched roofs. It celebrates craft heritage and artisan traditions – the opening show featured more than 1,000 shadow puppets. *218 Nanshan Lu, Shangcheng, www.caa.edu.cn*

Sifang Art Museum, Nanjing

Father and son real-estate moguls Lu Jun and Lu Xun pumped more than $150m into Sifang Art Museum. It peers out from the canopy of Laoshan forest at the entrance to a cultural complex with more than 20 pavilions designed by big names, including Ai Weiwei and David Adjaye. Steven Holl took on the museum project and defied the white-cube convention with a rectangular promenade. From ground-level galleries in dark, bamboo-formed concrete, you climb 30m to the 'floating' floor, which is clad in polycarbonate, allowing light to permeate the snaking corridors (Luc Tuymans' *Driver*, opposite, from the inaugural show 'The Garden of Diversion'); as do large picture windows. Closed Mondays and Tuesdays. It is less than two hours by train to Nanjing.
9 Zhenqi Lu, Pukou, T 025 5860 9999, www.sifangartmuseum.org

Suzhou Museum

Architect IM Pei's homage to his ancestral home evokes contemporary aesthetics while drawing on its ancient culture – this was the art and literary centre of China from the Song to the Qing dynasties. The whitewashed walls and tiled roofs of old Suzhou are reinterpreted as white facades framed in black granite, and octagonal and hexagonal shapes inspired by traditional gardens appear in light fixtures, apertures and water features. The gallery focuses on painting and calligraphy, including vital works by the Four Ming Masters, who were all from Suzhou. Other exhibitions display Buddhist scripture, pottery, textiles and silk, and jade and bronze antiquities from the Neolithic and Bronze Age sites around the city. Also worth a visit is the adjacent Zhong Wang Fu, a preserved 19th-century palace, and the 16th-century Garden of the Humble Administrator (T 0512 962 015).
204 Dongbei Lu, Gusu, T 0512 6757 5666, www.szmuseum.com

Blossom Hill Inn, Zhouzhuang

Picturesque Zhouzhuang is renowned for its extensive canals, which are hemmed by exquisitely engraved revetments and mooring stones. Many of the houses here date from the Ming and Qing dynasties and are still in use today. Thomas Dariel has interwoven three properties to create the 20-suite (Deluxe Garden View Room, above) Blossom Hill Inn. Original carved wood beams and screens, bamboo beds and copper details now meld seamlessly with graphic tiling and joyful furniture; the lighting is by modern Chinese designers. There's also a stylish library, fitted with a fireplace, as well as two dining spaces. It's an hour-and-a-half drive from Shanghai; if you can, visit in either spring or autumn, when the water town is particularly scenic. *110 Zhongshi Lu, T 0512 5722 0008, www.blossomhillinn.com*

02L · 5014 · 1194

138 · 1096 · 9651

Flair. Bar. superpotato

Fuyoe Antique Market
IAPM Mall · Probably Not

Xintiandi Style

1930 Can't Find

Art Deco M50 (Closed Mon)

RESOURCES
CITY GUIDE DIRECTORY

A

Aegis 088
1 Taojiang Lu
T 5419 8226
www.projectaegis.com

Alter 081
Shop L116
Xintiandi Style
245 Madang Lu
T 6302 9889
www.alterstyle.com

Anantara Spa 054
The PuLi Hotel and Spa
1 Changde Lu
T 3203 9999
www.thepuli.com

Annabel Lee 080
No 1
Lane 8
Zhongshan Dong Yi Lu
T 6445 8218
www.annabel-lee.com

Arcade 032
2nd floor
57 Fuxing Xilu
T 1670 0335
www.arcadesh.com

B

Banmoo 082
Room B122
258 Wending Lu
Xuhui
T 6128 5818
www.banmoo.cn

BaoBao 033
380 Shanxi Nanlu

Baoism 033
150 Hubin Lu B2/E30
T 6333 5676

Le Baron 040
7th floor
20 Donghu Lu
T 6483 2061
www.lebaronshanghai.com

Bar Rouge 032
7th floor
18 Zhongshan Dong Yi Lu
T 6339 1199
www.bar-rouge-shanghai.com

Benwu Studio 056
Suite 1401
Building 2
1728 Huangxing Lu
Yangpu
T 136 4620 5249
www.benwustudio.com

Boxing Cat Brewery 038
82 Fuxing Xilu
T 6431 2091
www.boxingcatbrewery.com

C

CAA Folk Art Museum 097
218 Nanshan Lu
Shangcheng
Hangzhou
www.caa.edu.cn

Calypso 037
Kerry Centre Piazza
Tongren Lu/An Yi Lu
T 2203 8888

Cantina Agave 038
291 Fumin Lu
T 6886 0706
www.cantinaagave.com

HOTELS
ADDRESSES AND ROOM RATES

Andaz 016
Room rates:
double, from ¥2,000
88 Songshan Lu
T 2310 1234
www.shanghai.andaz.hyatt.com

Blossom Hill Inn 102
Room rates:
double, from ¥680;
Deluxe Garden View Room, from ¥880
110 Zhongshi Lu
Zhouzhuang
T 0512 5722 0008
www.blossomhillinn.com

Cachet Boutique 022
Room rates:
double, from ¥1,300;
JG La Vie Balcony Suite, from ¥2,800;
Panache Penthouse, from ¥8,800
931 Nanjing Xilu (entrance on Taixing Lu)
T 6217 9000
www.cachethotels.com

Fairmont Peace Hotel 072
Room rates:
double, from ¥2,250
20 Nanjing Donglu
T 6138 6888
www.fairmont.com

Fuchun Resort 096
Room rates:
double, from ¥2,700
339 Jiangbin Dong Dadao
Fuyang
Hangzhou
T 0571 6346 1111
www.fuchunresort.com

JW Marriott 013
Room rates:
double, from ¥1,650
399 Nanjing Xilu
T 5359 4969
www.marriott.com

Langham 016
Room rates:
double, from ¥2,200
99 Madang Lu
T 2330 2288
www.langhamhotels.com

Naked Stables 096
Room rates:
double, from ¥2,200
37 Shangxiazhuang Village
Paitou
Moganshan
T 6431 8901
www.nakedretreats.cn

Park Hotel 077
Room rates:
double, from ¥1,150
170 Nanjing Xilu
T 6327 5225
www.parkhotelshanghai.cn

Park Hyatt 021
Room rates:
double, from ¥5,500;
Chairman Suite, from ¥73,500
SWFC
100 Century Avenue
T 6888 1234
www.parkhyattshanghai.com

The Peninsula 020
Room rates:
double, from ¥2,500;
Deluxe River Suite, from ¥7,400
32 Zhongshan Dong Yi Lu
T 2327 2888
www.peninsula.com

The Portman Ritz-Carlton 016
Room rates:
double, from ¥1,500
Shanghai Centre
1376 Nanjing Xilu
T 6279 8888
www.ritzcarlton.com

The PuLi Hotel and Spa 016
Room rates:
double, from ¥2,000
1 Changde Lu
T 3203 9999
www.thepuli.com

Shangri-La 016
Room rates:
double, from ¥1,600
33 Fu Cheng Lu
T 6882 8888
www.shangri-la.com

The Swatch Art Peace Hotel 017
Room rates:
double, from ¥3,500;
Happiness Suite, from ¥31,500;
Peace Suite, from ¥31,500
23 Nanjing Donglu
T 2329 8500
www.swatch-art-peace-hotel.com

Twelve at Hengshan 016
Room rates:
double, from ¥1,800
12 Hengshan Lu
T 3338 3888
www.starwoodhotels.com

Urbn 023
Room rates:
double, from ¥1,400;
Garden View, from ¥1,650
183 Jiaozhou Lu
T 5153 4600
www.urbnhotels.com

Waldorf Astoria 016
Room rates:
double, from ¥2,500
2 Zhongshan Dong Yi Lu
T 6322 9988
www.waldorfastoriashanghai.com

The Waterhouse 018
Room rates:
double, from ¥1,300;
Courtyard Suite, from ¥2,700
1-3 Maojiayuan Lu
South Bund
T 6080 2988
www.waterhouseshanghai.com

WALLPAPER* CITY GUIDES

Executive Editor
Jeremy Case

Author
Lillian He

Deputy Editor
Belle Place

**Contributing
Photography Editor**
Nabil Butt

Photography Editor
Rebecca Moldenhauer

Junior Art Editor
Jade R Arroyo

Editorial Assistants
Catalina L Imizcoz
Elena Gusperti

Intern
Mandy Tie

Production Controller
Nick Seston

Wallpaper*® is a
registered trademark
of Time Inc (UK)

First published 2006
Sixth edition 2017

© Phaidon Press Limited

All prices and venue
information are correct
at time of going to press,
but are subject to change.

Original Design
Loran Stosskopf
Map Illustrator
Russell Bell

Contacts
wcg@phaidon.com
@wallpaperguides

More City Guides
www.phaidon.com/travel

Phaidon Press Limited
Regent's Wharf
All Saints Street
London N1 9PA

Phaidon Press Inc
65 Bleecker Street
New York, NY 10012

Phaidon® is a registered
trademark of Phaidon
Press Limited

www.phaidon.com

A CIP Catalogue record for
this book is available from
the British Library.

Printed in China

ISBN 978 0 7148 7376 3

PHOTOGRAPHERS

SHANGHAI
A COLOUR-CODED GUIDE TO THE HOT 'HOODS

JING'AN
The downtown financial district teems with high-rises and salarymen letting off steam

XINTIANDI
This Disney-does-dining pleasure quarter proves that heritage isn't what it used to be

THE BUND
The epicentre of the city's Western past now looks to Western retailers for its future

FRENCH CONCESSION
Enjoy the mishmash of historic architecture, from art deco decadence to colonial chic

PUDONG
Come here for a lesson in how you turn farmland into a new Dubai in just two decades

PEOPLE'S PARK
The cultural hub of a commercial city, this is a good place to ease yourself into Shanghai

For a full description of each neighbourhood, see the Introduction.
Featured venues are colour-coded, according to the district in which they are located.